Bridgestone
B O O K S

Weather Update

Tornadoes

by Nathan Olson

Consultant:
Joseph M. Moran, PhD
Associate Director, Education Program
American Meteorological Society
Washington, D.C.

Capstone
press

Mankato, Minnesota

Bridgestone Books are published by Capstone Press,
151 Good Counsel Drive, P.O. Box 669, Mankato, Minnesota 56002.
www.capstonepress.com

Library of Congress Cataloging-in-Publication Data
Olson, Nathan.
Tornadoes / by Nathan Olson.
    p. cm.—(Bridgestone books. Weather update)
    Summary: "A brief introduction to tornadoes, including what they are, how they form,
and tornado safety"—Provided by publisher.
    Includes bibliographical references and index.
    ISBN 0-7368-4333-7 (hardcover)
    1. Tornadoes—Juvenile literature. I. Title. II. Series.
QC955.2.O38 2006
551.55'3—dc22   2004029587

Editorial Credits
Jennifer Besel, editor; Molly Nei, set designer; Kate Opseth, book designer; Wanda Winch,
    photo researcher; Scott Thoms, photo editor

Photo Credits
Capstone Press/Karon Dubke, 18 (foreground)
Digital Vision/Jim Reed, 1
Folio, Inc./David R. Frazier Photolibrary, 10; Everett C. Johnson, 16
Getty Images Inc./Alan R. Moller, cover
Peter Arnold, Inc./Gene Rhoden, 20; Weatherstock, 14
Photo Researchers, Inc./Katherine Bay and Jim Reed, 4
Unicorn Stock Photos/Jim Shippee, 18 (background); Martha McBride, 12
Visuals Unlimited/Chuck Doswell, 8

1 2 3 4 5 6 10 09 08 07 06 05

Table of Contents

4

What Are Tornadoes?

Lightning flashes across the sky. Hail pounds the ground. Black clouds form a **funnel**. As the tornado spins and twists, it sounds like a speeding train. This dangerous storm rips apart houses, trees, and cars.

A tornado is a spinning column of air. It reaches from the clouds to the ground. A tornado makes some of the fastest winds on earth. Winds in a tornado can blow more than 250 miles (400 kilometers) per hour.

◄ A huge tornado sweeps across a dirt road as police watch the direction of the storm.

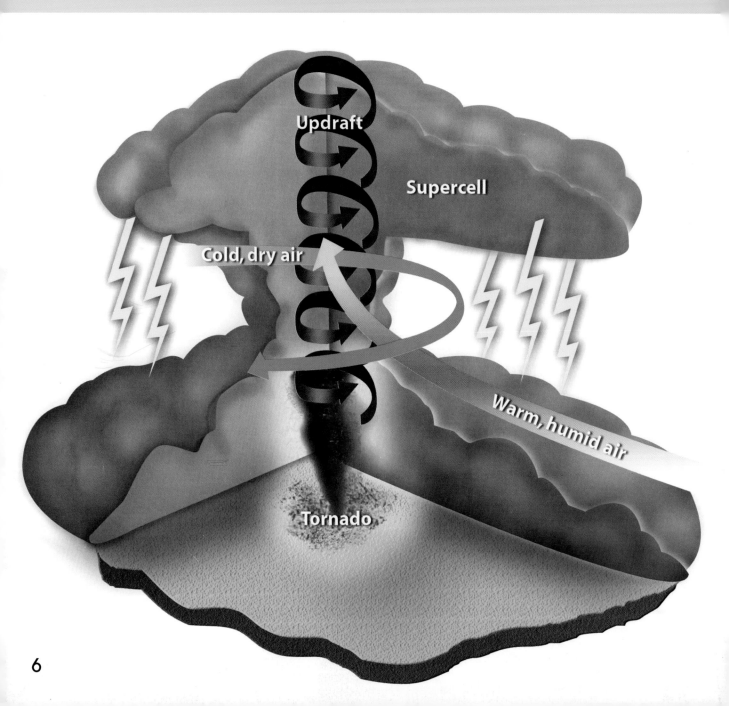

How Tornadoes Form

Many tornadoes form during strong thunderstorms called **supercells**. Supercells form when cold, dry air meets warm, **humid** air. The warm air climbs over the colder air. This rising air is called an **updraft**.

Strong winds make the rising updraft spin. As the air spins, it forms a funnel cloud. If the spinning funnel cloud stretches to the ground, it becomes a tornado.

◀ Inside the thunderstorm, rising air creates an updraft. Strong winds spin the air and form a tornado.

Where Tornadoes Happen

Tornadoes are most common in the United States. The United States has between 700 and 1,100 tornadoes each year. Most happen in Tornado Alley. Nebraska, Kansas, Oklahoma, and Texas make up Tornado Alley. The air and winds change quickly in this area. These changes can cause storms and tornadoes to form.

Tornadoes also happen in other parts of the world. They are common in Australia. Thunderstorms in Canada have also formed tornadoes.

◄ A tornado spins and twists across fields in Texas.

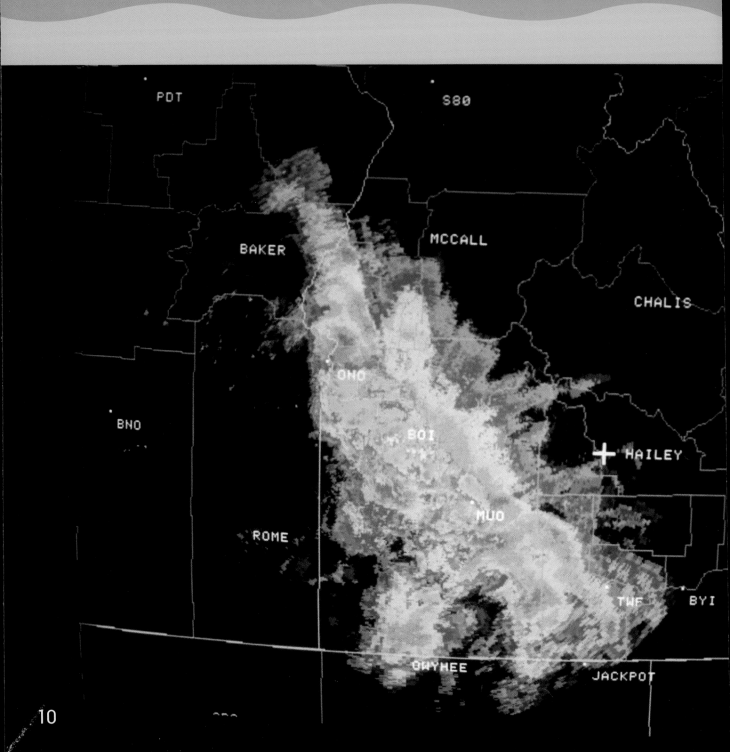

Forecasting Tornadoes

Tornadoes are hard to **forecast**. Forecasters use **Doppler radar** to look for tornadoes. The radar can show spinning air in a storm. Doppler radar can spot funnel clouds up to 25 minutes before they touch the ground.

Satellite pictures also help forecasters watch for tornadoes. Forecasters look for long, narrow groups of thunderstorms, called squall lines. Tornadoes often form out of these storms.

◀ Doppler radar images are color coded to help forecasters spot areas of heavy rainfall and possible tornadoes.

Measuring Tornadoes

The strength of a tornado is measured on the Fujita Tornado Scale, or F-scale. This scale measures wind speeds and damage from a tornado. Scientists use this scale to describe the force of a tornado.

The F-scale goes from F0 to F5. An F0 tornado is the weakest on the scale. These storms cause the least damage. An F5 is the strongest tornado. These tornadoes bring winds of at least 261 miles (420 kilometers) per hour. Some F5 tornadoes are strong enough to lift houses off the ground.

◄ Even weak F1 tornadoes can cause damage to power lines and roofs.

Tornado Season

Tornadoes can happen at any time of year. In the United States, tornadoes most often hit in spring. In spring, the air and winds can change quickly. Thunderstorms develop because of the weather changes. Tornadoes can form out of these thunderstorms.

May is the most common month for tornadoes. May 2003 set a record with 516 tornadoes. Many tornadoes also happen in April and June.

◀ Changing weather conditions in the spring often cause thunderstorms and tornadoes to form.

Waterspouts and Dust Devils

Spinning funnels of air are not always tornadoes. Waterspouts form on lakes or oceans. They are weaker than tornadoes. Waterspouts can suck up fish and blow them miles away.

A dust devil is a spinning mass of dusty air. Dust devils do not come from clouds. They can form anywhere there is hot, dry land. Wind lifts dust off the ground and spins it. Large dust devils can cause damage to land and buildings.

◀ A waterspout forms over the ocean near Key West, Florida.

Tornado Safety

The National Weather Service (NWS) warns when tornadoes may hit. NWS messages are read on TV and the radio. A tornado watch means a tornado is possible. A tornado warning means one has been seen by an **eyewitness** or on radar.

During a tornado, people need to go to a safe place. People should not go outside during a tornado. They should go to the basement or a room with no windows. They should have flashlights, radios, and batteries ready in case the power goes out.

◀ Forecasters give weather information on TV when watches and warnings are put out.

Major Tornadoes in History

On May 3, 1999, a powerful F5 tornado hit Oklahoma City. This tornado had winds that reached 318 miles (512 kilometers) per hour. Houses and cars were sucked off the ground.

An F5 tornado hit Jarrell, Texas, on May 27, 1997. It ripped up roads and trees. This huge tornado was nearly 1 mile (1.6 kilometers) wide. At least 27 people died.

Tornadoes are dangerous storms. Being prepared for a tornado is the best way to stay safe.

◄ The F5 tornado in Oklahoma City destroyed almost everything in its path.

Glossary

Doppler radar (DAWP-ler RAY-dar)—an instrument that uses microwaves to locate tornadoes

eyewitness (eye-WIT-niss)—someone who has seen something and can describe what happened

forecast (FOR-kast)—to say what you think will happen to the weather

funnel (FUHN-uhl)—an open cone that narrows to a tube

humid (HYOO-mid)—damp or moist

satellite (SAT-uh-lite)—a spacecraft that circles earth

supercell (SOO-pur-sel)—a powerful thunderstorm

updraft (UHP-draft)—a current of rising air

Read More

Spilsbury, Louise, and Richard Spilsbury. *Terrifying Tornadoes.* Awesome Forces of Nature. Chicago: Heinemann, 2004.

White, Matt. *Storm Chasers: On the Trail of Deadly Tornadoes.* High Five Reading. Mankato, Minn.: Capstone Curriculum, 2003.

Internet Sites

FactHound offers a safe, fun way to find Internet sites related to this book. All of the sites on FactHound have been researched by our staff.

Here's how:
1. Visit *www.facthound.com*
2. Type in this special code **0736843337** for age-appropriate sites. Or enter a search word related to this book for a more general search.
3. Click on the **Fetch It** button.

FactHound will fetch the best sites for you!

Index